# Walsh

### by Iain Gray

PUBLISHING

WRITING *to* REMEMBER

# Lang**Syne**

**PUBLISHING**

WRITING *to* REMEMBER

Vineyard Business Centre,
Pathhead, Midlothian EH37 5XP
Tel: 01875 321 203 Fax: 01875 321 233
E-mail: info@lang-syne.co.uk
www.langsyneshop.co.uk

Design by Dorothy Meikle
Printed by Montgomery Litho, Glasgow
© Lang Syne Publishers Ltd 2010

ISBN 978-1-85217-276-3

# Walsh

**MOTTO:**
Firm.

**CREST:**
A mailed arm, the hand
clutching a spear.

**NAME** variations include:
Branagh
Brannagh
Walch
Wallace
Wallis
Walshe
Welch
Welsh

*Chapter one:*
# Origins of Irish surnames

**According to an old saying, there are two types of Irish – those who actually are Irish and those who wish they were.**

This sentiment is only one example of the allure that the high romance and drama of the proud nation's history holds for thousands of people scattered across the world today.

It's a sad fact, however, that the vast majority of Irish surnames are found far beyond Irish shores, rather than on the Emerald Isle itself.

The population stood at around eight million souls in 1841, but today it stands at fewer than six million.

This is mainly a tragic consequence of the potato famine, also known as the Great Hunger, which devastated Ireland between 1845 and 1849.

The Irish peasantry had become almost wholly reliant for basic sustenance on the potato, first introduced from the Americas in the seventeenth century.

When the crop was hit by a blight, at least 800,000 people starved to death while an estimated two million others were forced to seek a new life far from their native shores – particularly in America, Canada, and Australia.

The effects of the potato blight continued until about 1851, by which time a firm pattern of emigration had become established.

Ireland's loss, however, was to the gain of the countries in which the immigrants settled, contributing enormously, as their descendants do today, to the well being of the nations in which their forefathers settled.

But those who were forced through dire circumstance to establish a new life in foreign parts never forgot their roots, or the proud heritage and traditions of the land that gave them birth.

Nor do their descendants.

It is a heritage that is inextricably bound up in the colourful variety of Irish names themselves – and the origin and history of these names forms an integral part of the vibrant drama that is the nation's history, one of both glorious fortune and tragic misfortune.

This history is well documented, and one of the most important and fascinating of the earliest sources are *The Annals of the Four Masters*, compiled between 1632 and 1636 by four friars at the Franciscan Monastery in County Donegal.

Compiled from earlier sources, and purporting to go back to the Biblical Deluge, much of the material takes in the mythological origins and history of Ireland and the Irish.

This includes tales of successive waves of invaders and settlers such as the Fomorians, the Partholonians, the Nemedians, the Fir Bolgs, the Tuatha De Danann, and the Laigain.

Of particular interest are the *Milesian Genealogies*,

because the majority of Irish clans today claim a descent from either Heremon, Ir, or Heber – three of the sons of Milesius, a king of what is now modern day Spain.

These sons invaded Ireland in the second millennium B.C, apparently in fulfilment of a mysterious prophecy received by their father.

This Milesian lineage is said to have ruled Ireland for nearly 3,000 years, until the island came under the sway of England's King Henry II in 1171 following what is known as the Cambro-Norman invasion.

This is an important date not only in Irish history in general, but for the effect the invasion subsequently had for Irish surnames.

'Cambro' comes from the Welsh, and 'Cambro-Norman' describes those Welsh knights of Norman origin who invaded Ireland.

But they were invaders who stayed, inter-marrying with the native Irish population and founding their own proud dynasties that bore Cambro-Norman names such as Archer, Barbour, Brannagh, Fitzgerald, Fitzgibbon, Fleming, Joyce, Plunkett, and Walsh – to name only a few.

These 'Cambro-Norman' surnames that still flourish throughout the world today form one of the three main categories in which Irish names can be placed – those of Gaelic-Irish, Cambro-Norman, and Anglo-Irish.

Previous to the Cambro-Norman invasion of the twelfth century, and throughout the earlier invasions and settlement of those wild bands of sea rovers known as the Vikings in the eighth and ninth centuries, the population of the island was relatively small, and it was normal for a person to be identified through the use of only a forename.

But as population gradually increased and there were many more people with the same forename, surnames were adopted to distinguish one person, or one community, from another.

Individuals identified themselves with their own particular tribe, or 'tuath', and this tribe – that also became known as a clann, or clan – took its name from some distinguished ancestor who had founded the clan.

The Gaelic-Irish form of the name Kelly, for example, is Ó Ceallaigh, or O'Kelly, indicating descent from an original 'Ceallaigh', with the 'O' denoting 'grandson of.' The name was later anglicised to Kelly.

The prefix 'Mac' or 'Mc', meanwhile, as with the clans of the Scottish Highlands, denotes 'son of.'

Although the Irish clans had much in common with their Scottish counterparts, one important difference lies in what are known as 'septs', or branches, of the clan.

Septs of Scottish clans were groups who often bore an entirely different name from the clan name but were under the clan's protection.

In Ireland, septs were groups that shared the same name and who could be found scattered throughout the four provinces of Ulster, Leinster, Munster, and Connacht.

The 'golden age' of the Gaelic-Irish clans, infused as their veins were with the blood of Celts, pre-dates the Viking invasions of the eighth and ninth centuries and the Norman invasion of the twelfth century, and the sacred heart of the country was the Hill of Tara, near the River Boyne, in County Meath.

Known in Gaelic as 'Teamhar na Rí', or Hill of Kings, it was the royal seat of the 'Ard Rí Éireann', or High King of Ireland, to whom the petty kings, or chieftains, from the island's provinces were ultimately subordinate.

It was on the Hill of Tara, beside a stone pillar known as the Irish 'Lia Fáil', or Stone of Destiny, that the High Kings were inaugurated and, according to legend, this stone would emit a piercing screech that could be heard all over Ireland when touched by the hand of the rightful king.

The Hill of Tara is today one of the island's main tourist attractions.

Opposition to English rule over Ireland, established in the wake of the Cambro-Norman invasion, broke out frequently and the harsh solution adopted by the powerful forces of the Crown was to forcibly evict the native Irish from their lands.

These lands were then granted to Protestant colonists, or 'planters', from Britain.

Many of these colonists, ironically, came from Scotland and were the descendants of the original 'Scotti', or 'Scots', who gave their name to Scotland after migrating there in the fifth century A.D., from the north of Ireland.

Colonisation entailed harsh penal laws being imposed on the majority of the native Irish population, stripping them practically of all of their rights.

The Crown's main bastion in Ireland was Dublin and its environs, known as the Pale, and it was the dispossessed peasantry who lived outside this Pale, desperately striving to eke out a meagre living.

It was this that gave rise to the modern-day expression of someone or something being 'beyond the pale'.

Attempts were made to stamp out all aspects of the ancient Gaelic-Irish culture, to the extent that even to bear a Gaelic-Irish name was to invite discrimination.

This is why many Gaelic-Irish names were anglicised with, for example, and noted above, Ó Ceallaigh, or O'Kelly, being anglicised to Kelly.

Succeeding centuries have seen strong revivals of Gaelic-Irish consciousness, however, and this has led to many families reverting back to the original form of their name, while the language itself is frequently found on the fluent tongues of an estimated 90,000 to 145,000 of the island's population.

Ireland's turbulent history of religious and political strife is one that lasted well into the twentieth century, a landmark century that saw the partition of the island into the twenty-six counties of the independent Republic of

Ireland, or Eire, and the six counties of Northern Ireland, or Ulster.

Dublin, originally founded by Vikings, is now a vibrant and truly cosmopolitan city while the proud city of Belfast is one of the jewels in the crown of Ulster.

It was Saint Patrick who first brought the light of Christianity to Ireland in the fifth century A.D.

Interpretations of this Christian message have varied over the centuries, often leading to bitter sectarian conflict – but the many intricately sculpted Celtic Crosses found all over the island are symbolic of a unity that crosses the sectarian divide.

It is an image that fuses the 'old gods' of the Celts with Christianity.

All the signs from the early years of this new millennium indicate that sectarian strife may soon become a thing of the past – with the Irish and their many kinsfolk across the world, be they Protestant or Catholic, finding common purpose in the rich tapestry of their shared heritage.

*Chapter two:*
# Invasion force

**Although the Walsh presence in Ireland dates back to no earlier than the Cambro-Norman invasion of the island in 1169, bearers of the name became so firmly rooted in the valleys and mountains of their adopted land that their exploits, trials, and tribulations, form an integral part of the rich fabric of the nation's often tumultuous history.**

The name, quite simply, means 'from Wales', although one Gaelic-Irish form of the name – Branagh, or Brannagh – stems from 'Breahnach', meaning a 'Breton', or a 'Welshman.'

Other forms of the name include Walch, Wallace, Wallis, Walshe, Welch, and Welsh.

The presence of the form 'Wallace' highlights an intriguing parallel between those original Welshmen of Norman stock who subsequently settled in Ireland and those Anglo-Normans who later settled in Scotland.

The Normans, from the French province of Normandy, first came to England in the wake of the Norman Conquest of 1066 in which King Harold was defeated at the battle of Hastings.

Many of William the Conqueror's followers were granted lands in the nation they had invaded, and later in Wales.

Under Scotland's David I, who ruled from 1124 to 1153, many Anglo-Norman landholders were encouraged to settle in Scotland – and these included the famed families of Wallace and Bruce.

Sir William Wallace, of course, is renowned as the great Scottish 'Braveheart' and freedom fighter against English oppression, while Robert the Bruce was the Scots king who won a memorable battle against the forces of England's Edward II at the battle of Bannockburn in 1314.

It was not long after the Anglo-Norman families settled in Scotland that they came to identify themselves with their new nation, becoming as 'Scottish' as the native Scots themselves.

A similar process occurred in Ireland, when the Norman invaders such as the Walshs became as 'Irish' as the native Irish.

This was a gradual process, however, and it was most definitely in the form of aggressive and ambitious invaders that the Walshs first arrived in Ireland.

Twelfth century Ireland was far from being a unified nation, split up as it was into territories ruled over by squabbling chieftains who ruled as kings in their own right – and this inter-clan rivalry worked to the advantage of the invaders.

In a series of bloody conflicts one chieftain, or king, would occasionally gain the upper hand over his rivals, and by 1156 the most powerful was Muirchertach MacLochlainn, king of the O'Neills.

He was opposed by Rory O'Connor, king of the province of Connacht, but he increased his power and influence by allying himself with Dermot MacMurrough, king of Leinster.

MacLochlainn and MacMurrough were aware that the main key to the kingdom of Ireland was the thriving trading port of Dublin that had been established by invading Vikings, or Ostmen, in 852 A.D.

Dublin was taken by the combined forces of the Leinster and Connacht kings, but when MacLochlainn died the Dubliners rose up in revolt and overthrew the unpopular MacMurrough.

A triumphant Rory O'Connor entered Dublin and was later inaugurated as Ard Rí, but MacMurrough refused to accept defeat.

He appealed for help from England's Henry II in unseating O'Connor, an act that was to radically affect the future course of Ireland's fortunes.

The English monarch agreed to help MacMurrough, but distanced himself from direct action by delegating his Norman subjects in Wales with the task.

With an eye on rich booty, plunder, and lands, they were only too eager to obey their sovereign's wishes.

MacMurrough rallied powerful barons such as Robert Fitzstephen and Maurice Fitzgerald to his cause, along with Gilbert de Clare, Earl of Pembroke, and seasoned fighters such as the Walshs.

The mighty Norman war machine soon moved into action, invading the island in 1169, and so fierce and disciplined was their onslaught on the forces of Rory O'Connor and his allies that by 1171 they had re-captured Dublin, in the name of MacMurrough, and other strategically important territories.

It was now that a nervous Henry II began to take cold feet over the venture, realising that he may have created a rival in the form of a separate Norman kingdom in Ireland.

Accordingly, he landed on the island, near Waterford, at the head of a large army in October of 1171 with the aim of curbing the power of his Cambro-Norman barons.

Protracted war between the king and his barons was averted, however, when they submitted to the royal will, promising homage and allegiance in return for holding the territories they had conquered in the king's name.

Henry also received the submission and homage of many of the Irish chieftains, tired as they were with internecine warfare and also perhaps realising that as long as they were rivals and not united they were no match for the powerful forces the English Crown could muster.

English dominion over Ireland was ratified through the Treaty of Windsor of 1175, while two years earlier Pope Alexander III had given Papal sanction to Henry's dominance over Ireland.

This was on condition that he uphold the rights of the Holy Roman Catholic Church and that chieftains adhere rigorously to the oaths of fealty they had sworn to the English king.

The crest on the coat of arms of the Walshs of Ireland features a mailed arm, with the hand clutching a spear, and the motto 'Firm.'

But an indication of the number of separate Walsh families who became established in Ireland in the wake of the invasion can be gained from the fact that there are several Walsh family coats of arms.

These include the Walshs of Ballykilcavan, in Co. Laois who, while bearing the motto 'Firm', have as their crest a griffin's head.

The crest of the Walshs of Castlehale, in Co. Kilkenny, is a swan pierced with an arrow, and their motto is 'Pierced but not dead', while the crest of the Walshs of Carrickmines, in Co. Dublin, is a demi-lion rampant and their intriguing motto is 'Do not irritate the lions.'

Walshs, in fact, were to be found all over Ireland: not only in the three counties referred to above, but scattered as far afield as Waterford, Wexford and Carlow, Kerry, Tipperary, Cork, Mayo, Louth, Galway, Roscommon, Limerick, Kildare and Meath, Westmeath, Offaly, Carlow, and Sligo.

The sheer geographical spread of these Walsh septs, or families, goes some way towards explaining the conflicting claims concerning whether or not they all originally sprang from the loins of the same progenitor.

One theory is that they have a common ancestor in 'Walynus', who came to Ireland in the military retinue of Maurice Fitzgerald: it was through this Walynus that the famed Walsh of the Mountains family, in south-central Co. Kilkenny, was established.

Other sources refer to 'Philip of Wales' (who could, perhaps, have been the same personage as Walynus), whose son, Howel, gave his name to the Walsh stronghold of Castle Hoel – also known as Castlehale, or Castlehowel.

Philip, also referred to by some sources as Philip Brenagh, is said to have taken part in a naval battle in 1174 against those Viking settlers known as the Ostmen.

Referred to as 'a young soldier of great prowess', he is hailed as having played a significant role in defeating the Ostmen.

Philip was granted a baronage as reward for his part in the invasion and subsequent subjugation of the island, while a David Le Walleys ('David of Wales') was rewarded with baronage of Carrickmines, near Dublin.

Another theory is that the Walshs who came to Ireland originated from the Pembrokeshire area, while another claim is that they may have enjoyed close family ties with the barons of Cornwall.

Yet another theory gives the Walshs of Ireland a truly illustrious pedigree – with a descent from Owen Gwynnes, a prince of north Wales.

If correct, this would certainly give the Walshs an ancient Celtic pedigree – and it is interesting to speculate that this may go some way towards explaining how they so readily assimilated with the native Celtic stock of Ireland.

*Chapter three:*

# Loss and lament

**Assimilation with the native Irish clans and their way of life involved a number of important marriage alliances, with the Walshs forging these with ancient clans such as the O'Rourkes, the O'Connors, the McCarthys, and the O'Donnells.**

But assimilation was destined to come at a fatal cost – as the events of succeeding centuries were to prove for not only the native Irish themselves, but those original Norman invaders such as the Walshs who rebelled against the increasing encroachment of the English Crown in their affairs.

Three separate 'nations' of Ireland had been created in the wake of the Norman invasion.

These were the territories of the privileged and powerful Norman barons and their retainers such as the Walshs, the Ireland of the disaffected Gaelic-Irish who held lands unoccupied by the Normans, and the Pale – comprised of Dublin itself and a substantial area of its environs ruled over by an English elite.

But, through time, the original Norman families and the native Irish would find common cause.

A simmering cauldron of discontent had been brewing for some time, and this boiled over in 1641 in the form of a rebellion by the Catholic landowners such as the Walshs against the English Crown's policy of settling, or 'planting' loyal Protestants on Irish land.

This policy had started during the reign from 1491 to 1547 of Henry VIII, whose Reformation effectively outlawed the established Roman Catholic faith throughout his dominions.

This settlement of loyal Protestants in Ireland continued throughout the subsequent reigns of Elizabeth I, James I (James VI of Scotland), and Charles I.

In the insurrection that exploded in 1641, at least 2,000 Protestant settlers were massacred at the hands of Catholic landowners and their native Irish peasantry, while thousands more were stripped of their belongings and driven from their lands to seek refuge where they could.

Terrible as the atrocities were against the Protestant settlers, subsequent accounts became greatly exaggerated, serving to fuel a burning desire on the part of Protestants for revenge against the rebels.

Tragically for Ireland, this revenge became directed not only against the rebels, but Irish Catholics such as the Walshs in general.

The English Civil War intervened to prevent immediate action against the rebels, but following the execution of Charles I in 1649 and the consolidation of the power of England's Oliver Cromwell, the time was ripe for revenge.

The Lord Protector, as he was named, descended on Ireland at the head of a 20,000-strong army that landed at Ringford, near Dublin, in August of 1649.

The consequences of this Cromwellian conquest still resonate throughout the island today.

Cromwell had three main aims: to quash all forms of rebellion, to 'remove' all Catholic landowners who had taken part in the rebellion, and to convert the native Irish to the Protestant faith.

An early warning of the terrors that were in store for the native Catholic Irish came when the north-eastern town of Drogheda was stormed and taken in September and between 2,000 and 4,000 of its inhabitants killed, including priests who were summarily put to the sword.

It was not long before Cromwell held Ireland in a grip of iron, allowing him to implement what amounted to a policy of ethnic cleansing.

His troopers were given free rein to hunt down and kill priests, while all Catholic estates were confiscated.

Grim memories of the Cromwellian conquest of Ireland and the truly devastating consequences it had for the Walshes are to be found in what is known as *The Caoine of Walter Oidhre Breathnach.*

This refers to a 'caoine', or lament, penned by John MacWalter Walsh, famed as the late sixteenth to mid seventeenth century 'Bard of the Mountain.'

Born at Inchnacarran, he was bard, or poet, to the

Walsh of the Mountains family, and women would normally have recited his lament in the native Irish tongue.

Lamenting the horrors visited upon the Walshs throughout the invasion and its aftermath, it begins:

*Assemble round, O dear children of my soul, ours is a sad tale of woe, and with sorrow shall be recounted; the harvest of death lies in sward, but no ripening shall perfect it.*

The verses end with the haunting line:

*The Walshs of the Mountain shall be wide dispersed and their power dissolved forever.*

The scale of suffering experienced by the Walshs was of devastating proportions.

As reprisal for taking up arms against Cromwell, the Walsh of the Mountains stronghold of Castlehale was besieged and taken in 1650 – with survivors executed where they stood and cast into a burial pit at the bottom of a hill near the castle.

Their pathetic remains were uncovered during road building near the hill in the early years of the nineteenth century.

The Walsh bastion of Carrickmines, south of Dublin, was stormed and blown up and its defenders put to the sword, while thousands of acres of other Walsh estates throughout the length and breadth of the island were confiscated.

In Co. Kilkenny alone, an estimated 18,000 acres of Walsh property were confiscated.

Walsh fortunes enjoyed a brief, but limited, revival following the restoration to the throne of Charles II in 1660, but all was lost again in what is known as the Williamite Campaign of 1689 to 1691, and its aftermath.

The birth of an heir to James II (James VII of Scotland) in 1688 and consequent fears of the Protestant magnates of both England and Ireland of a Catholic restoration led to the Protestant Prince William of Orange being offered the throne.

William took up the offer as James fled into exile in France – but with French support he arrived at Kinsale in March of 1689 with the hope of wresting back his throne.

In this endeavour he had the support not only of the French, but loyal Catholic supporters in Ireland, such as the Walshs.

Despite some initial successes, however, his cause was ultimately doomed.

William landed at Carrickfergus and defeated James at the battle of the Boyne on July 12, 1690, and James was again forced to flee into exile – this time never to return.

The Williamite forces subsequently took Dublin and Athlone, and final Jacobite defeat (with 'Jacobite' indicating support for the deposed Stuart monarch, James) came following defeats at Aughrim, Galway, and Limerick.

Under the Treaty of Limerick of October 1691 some Irish officers who had served the Jacobite cause were allowed to leave for exile in France, while in Ireland itself harsh penal laws were implemented against the Catholic population.

These included, in 1695, legislation that restricted the rights of Catholics in not only education, but also in the ownership of horses, while the Catholic clergy were banned outright.

Further laws were passed to restrict the rights of Catholics to hold public office and in landholding, while in 1728 an Act was passed that withdrew the right of Catholics to vote.

Smarting under this oppression many Catholics, such as the Walshs, literally voted with their feet and sought a new life on distant shores in the service of foreign armies such as those of France or Spain – any country, in fact that was at war with Britain.

During the American Revolutionary War from 1775 to 1783 against Britain, one of the most famous regiments was Walsh's Regiment of the Irish Brigade (of France), which served the American cause under the command of Count Charles d'Estaing.

Many Walshs remained staunch Jacobites – including Antoine Walsh, a French naval officer born at St. Malo in 1703 and who was a son of the Irish-born shipbuilder Philip Walsh.

Walsh senior commanded the vessel that brought James II to exile in France, while his son helped to furnish arms and shipping for Charles Edward Stuart, better known to posterity as Bonnie Prince Charlie, for the Jacobite Rising of 1745.

This was a Rising that ended in the virtual extinction of any hopes of a Stuart restoration in the carnage of the battle of Culloden in May of 1746.

Far from the battlefield, however, generations of Walshs have found fame and fortune in rather more constructive pursuits

*Chapter four:*

# On the world stage

**Despite being first released more than fifty years ago, the film *The Quiet Man* still acts as a major incentive for tourists to visit Ireland, with thousands flocking to the island every year inspired by its rich evocation of the island's lush landscape.**

Had it not been for the pen of an Irish novelist by the name of **Maurice Walsh**, however, the movie would never have been made.

Born in Lisselton, near Listowel, Co. Kerry, in 1879, Walsh wrote *The Quiet Man* as a short story for the Saturday Evening Post in 1933.

The story was spotted by the noted Hollywood film director John Ford, who was so impressed that he bought the film rights from Walsh – for the rather unimpressive sum, considering the film's huge success, of $10.

It took Ford a number of years to obtain the necessary financial backing to make the film, but his faith was justified when it hit the movie screens across the world in 1952.

Starring John Wayne, Victor McLaglen, Maureen O'Hara, and Barry Fitzgerald, it was shot mainly in Cong, Co. Mayo, in the grounds of Ashford Castle and featured many ordinary Irish folk as film extras.

It was nominated for no less than seven Oscars, with

Ford winning an Oscar for best director, and Archie Stout and Winton C. Hoch taking the award for best cinematography.

A veteran of many films, John Wayne nevertheless maintained to the end of his days that of all the films in which he starred, *The Quiet Man* was his favourite.

The unassuming Maurice Walsh died in 1964.

On the contemporary stage, **Mary Walsh** is the actress and comedian born in St. Johns, Newfoundland, in 1952, and who won Best Supporting Actress at the Atlantic Film Festival in 1992 for her role in *Secret Nation*.

In 2006 she and Ed MacDonald gained a Canadian Gemini Award for best writing in a comedy or variety programme for their work on *Hatching, Matching, and Dispatching*, while she is also a prominent spokesperson for Oxfam Canada's campaign on human rights.

**Kate Walsh**, born San Jose, California, in 1967, is the television actress and star of the American series *Grey's Anatomy*, while **Kay Walsh**, born in London in 1911 and who died in 2005, was the English actress and dancer who appeared in films that include Alfred Hitchcock's *Stage Fright*, and Noel Coward's *In Which We Serve* and *This Happy Breed*.

Born in San Francisco in 1953, **J.T. Walsh** was the veteran American film star who had memorable roles in films that include *Good Morning Vietnam*, and *A Few Good Men*. He died in 1998.

**William J. Walsh**, born in 1957, has the unusual distinction of being not only a fire-fighter, but an American actor famous for his role in the television series *Third Watch*, where he started as a fire-fighting consultant.

At the time of writing he is captain of the Fire Department of New York Squad H, in the city's Bronx.

In the world of film production and screenwriting, **Bill Walsh**, born in New York in 1913 and who died in 1975, worked mainly on Walt Disney film productions including *Mary Poppins*, for which he shared Oscars for both best picture and for best writing and screenplay.

New Zealand-born **Fran Walsh** is the talented screenwriter, film producer, and musician who, along with her partner, filmmaker Peter Jackson, was responsible for the Oscar award-winning *Lord of the Rings* trilogy of movies, released between 2001 and 2003.

As a musician, she composed two haunting songs for the last in the trilogy, *Return of the King – Into the West* and *A Shadow Lies Between Us*.

Also in the world of music, **Craig Walsh** is a contemporary American composer, born in Somerville, New Jersey, in 1971, and whose many awards to date include a prestigious Guggenheim Fellowship.

In the world of contemporary rock music, **Joe Walsh**, born Wichita, Kansas, in 1947 is the guitarist and songwriter who enjoyed a successful career with *The James Gang*, and an equally successful solo career before achieving superstardom status through his membership of *The Eagles*.

**Kimberley Walsh**, born in Bradford, West Yorkshire, in 1981, is a singer with the highly successful British pop group *Girls Aloud*, while on the business side of the music industry **Louis Walsh**, born in Kiltimagh, Co. Mayo, in 1952, has achieved a total of 29 U.K. Number One singles to date through his management of acts that have included *Girls Aloud*, *Westlife*, and *Boyzone*.

He is a judge on the talent show *The X Factor*, the British equivalent of *American Idol*.

Tragic circumstances lie behind what propelled **John E. Walsh**, born in Auburn, New York, in 1945, to American television fame.

Host of the TV show *America's Most Wanted*, he became a committed anti-crime activist following the murder of his six-year-old son, Adam, after he was abducted from a department store near his home in Florida.

In the highly competitive world of sport, **Matt Walsh**, born in Holland, Pennsylvania, in 1982, is a top American professional basketball player, while **Kerri Walsh**, born in California in 1978, is the American beach volleyball player who, along with Misty May, took a gold medal for women's beach volleyball in the 2004 Olympics.

On the cricket field, **Courtney Walsh**, born Kingstown, Jamaica, in 1962, is the former international fast bowler who represented the West Indies from 1984 to 2001, and captained the side in no less than 22 Test Matches.

**Bill Walsh**, born in 1931, and a former head coach of the San Francisco 49ers and Stanford University, is recognised as one of the greatest innovators in the game of American football.

Born in Plains, Pennsylvania, in 1881, **Ed Walsh** was an American Major League Baseball player who was inducted into the Baseball Hall of Fame in 1946 and who is ranked among the nation's greatest ever players.

In the realms of international diplomacy, **Father Edmund A. Walsh**, who was born in 1885 and died in 1956, was the American Jesuit priest who was motivated to help form the Georgetown University's School of Foreign Service in the aftermath of the First World War.

Father Walsh had become disillusioned at the wrangling of the foreign powers at the Versailles Peace Conference of 1919 and the obvious lack of experience of many diplomats.

He became professor of geopolitics at the School of Foreign Service and, among other important international duties, directed the Papal Famine Relief Mission to Russia in 1922.

The highly respected priest and expert on geopolitics also played an important role as consultant to the U.S. Chief of Counsel at the Nuremberg War Crimes Trials in the aftermath of the Second World War.

**Evalyn Walsh McLean**, born in Leadville, Colorado, in 1886, achieved notoriety for a rather more sedentary career as an American mining heiress and socialite.

The only daughter of **Thomas Walsh**, an Irish immigrant and miner who literally struck it rich, she became the last private owner of the famed Star of the East diamond and the Hope diamond, thanks to the fabulous wealth accrued by her father.

They say that money attracts money, and this was no less so the case than in 1908 when Evalyn married Edward Beale McLean, heir to the *Washington Post* and *Cincinnati Enquirer* newspaper publishing empire.

The couple do not appear to have been born with the hard-working genes of their respective fathers, however, and soon became the talk of society for their very public spats, frequently fuelled by the large amounts of alcohol consumed by Edward and the morphine to which Evalyn became addicted.

Their notoriety even found expression in song – in the form of Cole Porter's *Anything Goes*, the title song of the highly popular 1934 musical. Evalyn died in 1947.

## *Key dates in Ireland's history from the first settlers to the formation of the Irish Republic:*

| | |
|---|---|
| **circa 7000 B.C.** | Arrival and settlement of Stone Age people. |
| **circa 3000 B.C.** | Arrival of settlers of New Stone Age period. |
| **circa 600 B.C.** | First arrival of the Celts. |
| **200 A.D.** | Establishment of Hill of Tara, Co. Meath, as seat of the High Kings. |
| **circa 432 A.D.** | Christian mission of St. Patrick. |
| **800-920 A.D.** | Invasion and subsequent settlement of Vikings. |
| **1002 A.D.** | Brian Boru recognised as High King. |
| **1014** | Brian Boru killed at battle of Clontarf. |
| **1169-1170** | Cambro-Norman invasion of the island. |
| **1171** | Henry II claims Ireland for the English Crown. |
| **1366** | Statutes of Kilkenny ban marriage between native Irish and English. |
| **1529-1536** | England's Henry VIII embarks on religious Reformation. |
| **1536** | Earl of Kildare rebels against the Crown. |
| **1541** | Henry VIII declared King of Ireland. |
| **1558** | Accession to English throne of Elizabeth I. |
| **1565** | Battle of Affane. |
| **1569-1573** | First Desmond Rebellion. |
| **1579-1583** | Second Desmond Rebellion. |
| **1594-1603** | Nine Years War. |
| **1606** | Plantation' of Scottish and English settlers. |
| **1607** | Flight of the Earls. |
| **1632-1636** | Annals of the Four Masters compiled. |
| **1641** | Rebellion over policy of plantation and other grievances. |
| **1649** | Beginning of Cromwellian conquest. |
| **1688** | Flight into exile in France of Catholic Stuart monarch James II as Protestant Prince William of Orange invited to take throne of England along with his wife, Mary. |
| **1689** | William and Mary enthroned as joint monarchs; siege of Derry. |
| **1690** | Jacobite forces of James defeated by William at battle of the Boyne (July) and Dublin taken. |

| | |
|---|---|
| **1691** | Athlone taken by William; Jacobite defeats follow at Aughrim, Galway, and Limerick; conflict ends with Treaty of Limerick (October) and Irish officers allowed to leave for France. |
| **1695** | Penal laws introduced to restrict rights of Catholics; banishment of Catholic clergy. |
| **1704** | Laws introduced constricting rights of Catholics in landholding and public office. |
| **1728** | Franchise removed from Catholics. |
| **1791** | Foundation of United Irishmen republican movement. |
| **1796** | French invasion force lands in Bantry Bay. |
| **1798** | Defeat of Rising in Wexford and death of United Irishmen leaders Wolfe Tone and Lord Edward Fitzgerald. |
| **1800** | Act of Union between England and Ireland. |
| **1803** | Dublin Rising under Robert Emmet. |
| **1829** | Catholics allowed to sit in Parliament. |
| **1845-1849** | The Great Hunger: thousands starve to death as potato crop fails and thousands more emigrate. |
| **1856** | Phoenix Society founded. |
| **1858** | Irish Republican Brotherhood established. |
| **1873** | Foundation of Home Rule League. |
| **1893** | Foundation of Gaelic League. |
| **1904** | Foundation of Irish Reform Association. |
| **1913** | Dublin strikes and lockout. |
| **1916** | Easter Rising in Dublin and proclamation of an Irish Republic. |
| **1917** | Irish Parliament formed after Sinn Fein election victory. |
| **1919-1921** | War between Irish Republican Army and British Army. |
| **1922** | Irish Free State founded, while six northern counties remain part of United Kingdom as Northern Ireland, or Ulster; civil war up until 1923 between rival republican groups. |
| **1949** | Foundation of Irish Republic after all remaining constitutional links with Britain are severed. |